when the
Rapture
comes

ESSENTIAL POETS SERIES 196

**Canada Council   Conseil des Arts
for the Arts   du Canada**

**ONTARIO ARTS COUNCIL
CONSEIL DES ARTS DE L'ONTARIO**

Guernica Editions Inc. acknowledges the support of
the Canada Council for the Arts and the Ontario Arts Council.
The Ontario Arts Council is an agency of the Government of Ontario.

when the
Rapture
comes

Max Layton

GUERNICA
TORONTO – BUFFALO – BERKELEY – LANCASTER (U.K.) 2012

Michael Mirolla, editor
Guernica Editions Inc.
P.O. Box 117, Station P, Toronto (ON), Canada M5S 2S6
2250 Military Road, Tonawanda, N.Y. 14150-6000 U.S.A.

Distributors:
University of Toronto Press Distribution,
5201 Dufferin Street, Toronto (ON), Canada M3H 5T8
Gazelle Book Services, White Cross Mills, High
Town, Lancaster LA1 4XS U.K.
Small Press Distribution, 1341 Seventh St.,
Berkeley, CA 94710-1409 U.S.A.

First edition.
Printed in Canada.

Legal Deposit – Third Quarter
Library of Congress Catalog Card Number: 2012938362
Library and Archives Canada Cataloguing in Publication

Layton, Max, 1946-
When the rapture comes / Max Layton.
(Essential poets series ; 196) Poems.
Issued also in electronic format.
ISBN 978-1-55071-642-9

I. Title. II. Series: Essential poets series ; 196

PS8623.A9483W54 2012   C811'.6   C2012-902907-6

For my wife, Sharon

The author describes the process of writing a villanelle (2:11)
www.tinyurl.com/RaptureVillanelle

TO SING ANOTHER VILLANELLE

To sing another villanelle
We climb or, drowning, die of thirst
At the bottom of this well

No fitter rhyme could this tale tell
For we, though last, are not the first
To sing another villanelle

When towers burned in sky-high hell
We found our world, ourselves, reversed
At the bottom of this well

When lovers jumped and others fell
Our parched hearts yearned, before they burst
To sing another villanelle

That sidewalk thump will sound our knell
Unless that sound, in art, is nursed
At the bottom of this well

Though words can never death dispel
Our spirits rise in verse un-hearsed
To sing another villanelle
At the bottom of this well

The author reads "To Sing Another Villanelle" (1:34)
www.tinyurl.com/RecitesVillanelle

Contents

REMEMBERING

When the rapture comes, they'll put
Humpty-Dumpty together again, along with
All the puzzles where the pieces
Didn't fit – my parents, for instance
My own disastrous marriage

The Jews of Auschwitz
Together with Hitler

Ukrainian kulaks and gulag zeks
Together with Stalin

Forty to sixty million Chinese
Together with Chairman Mao

Cambodians

Vietnamese boat people who never made it

The victims of 9/11

The sky a vast blue dome
With a gigantic crack in it
Shafts of silvery golden light
Beaming everybody up

Limbs hurtling towards
Their owners' bodies
Severed arms, legs, heads
Van Gogh's ear
Bits and pieces swirling all around us

The air thick with the blood of remembering

The author reads "Remembering" (1:31)
www.tinyurl.com/RecitesRemembering

SOME SMALL CEREMONY

When the rapture comes, there will surely
Be some recompense, some acknowledgement
Some small ceremony for those of us who
Never compromised, who never signed on
Who never pulled the simple trick that would
Have made us rich and famous, who refused
To light the boss's cigarette, who stuck by wives
And stupid husbands, who muttered no when
The answer obviously was yes, who toiled away
In obscurity and never achieved a thing
Martyrs, misfits, and heretics, our strange
Spirits distilled in our own alembic fires
I believe some day there will be some small
Ceremony for all us angels with broken wings

WITH MY ROUGH FINGERS

When the rapture comes
The good-looking girls
In Tim Horton's will talk to me
Sit down at my table
Ask polite, intelligent questions
About the book I am reading
Sensing the exquisite loneliness
Of my soul
They will unbutton
Their blouses
Let me admire the milk-white beauty
Of their breasts
Let me caress
With my rough fingers
Their golden feathered wings

The author reads "With My Rough Fingers" (0:59)
www.tinyurl.com/RecitesRoughFingers

LIFE WORK

When the rapture comes
Everybody's family will be reunited
My parents' heads suddenly haloed
By the sunlit windshield of their
Black-hooded Hudson, the stick-shift
Mounted on the floor
Angling upwards between them

My mother young again
The way I remember
Her eyes like Ingrid Bergman's
My father somewhere in his thirties
His hair black and thick

He is whispering the words
Of his newest poem, over and
Over, his fingers tapping out the
Rhythm on the steering wheel

My mother is staring stonily, angrily
Straight ahead, not saying anything

Her paintings are piled high on the roof
Of the car, this time her life work tied
Securely, so as not to be burned in a fire
At the Four Penny Art Gallery in Montreal
Or blown into the sea somewhere
Off the coast of Big Sur, California

There's a huge box of my father's
More than fifty books
On the back seat beside me
I myself am standing on the seat
Jumping up and down
Or, if I am no longer a child
Maybe just sitting there
Holding this book of my own

WAITING FOR THE RAPTURE

When the rapture comes, the trip to
Lockeport, Nova Scotia, will take
Less than a minute

As it is, I've been carrying
My mother's ashes all the way
From California
Since 1984

This is 2011
You do the math

In a cardboard box
With Frances Elizabeth Layton
And the name of the mortuary
Stenciled on the top

Naturally, the guard
At the Canada-U.S. border
Thought I was smuggling dope

You should have seen
The look on his face
When he opened the box
Reached in with gotcha glee
And his hand came out holding
Human bone

After that, carted from house
To house through several moves
Ending at the back of a filing cabinet
Where it stayed the last twenty years

Ashes gathering dust

The kind of joke
My mother might have made

Then a long walk along the beach
Carrying the box to Splash Rock
An outcrop at the southern end
The same place she told me
She used to sit as a kid

The sea surging
Sucking at the kelp
The water turning white for
Less than a minute

FATHERS AND SONS

When the rapture comes this memory
Will still remain: two men
Standing in a river, father and son
Throwing a tennis ball back and forth
On a beautiful summer day
With a breeze strong enough
To keep the bugs away

The father throwing the ball
High and headed straight downwind
The son leaping, returning the throw
With all his strength, the ball falling
Short, the current bringing it back
To the son again and again

INTIMATIONS OF MORTALITY

When the rapture comes
You won't see that look any more
That look my dad had
When he turned eighty

Part envy, part pride
A flicker of resentment
At the sight of my young man's
Muscles, elastic skin
The possibility of mistresses

The braggadocio behind my
Suggestion that he ought to
Exercise more often

My laughter when he tried
To touch his toes

I remember the look he gave me
When, for the first time, my
Interpretation of a movie
Was better than his

I remember my feeling of triumph
Together with the guilty knowledge
That I had pushed too hard

That my victory had been too easy

I remember him sitting at the table
His boxer's chin tucked in
His forehead towards me
His white hair thinning

Ironic, self-deprecating, almost
Apologetic, the look came from
Deep within

An indomitable spirit stuck in a body
That was giving up

A son struck by his father's look
Of wrinkled amazement

ALZHEIMER'S

When the rapture comes, my father
Who died of Alzheimer's
Will remember me

However, here in the Here Before
It is frightening to see how quickly
The disremembering has begun

First his body

His blue eyes
Those intensely searching eyes
His black eyebrows
The ones he got from his mother
His nose, chin, mouth
That eloquent mouth

Then his clothes

Donated
Perhaps worn now by the homeless

His watch

Stolen
From his room in the old folks' home
Along with a few cheap rings

His five charred, chewed pipes
Dispersed among his children

His library

Sold for a pittance because
Nobody reads books these days

His papers, letters, manuscripts

Sold for considerably more
To a university in Saskatchewan

Finally his memory

No plaque or statue at York University
Where he was professor of Eng Lit

Nothing at Guelph or U of T
Where he was writer-in-residence

Nothing in Montreal
Where he grew up in a slum
And lived most of his life

A tiny street named after him
In the suburb of Cote St Luc

A small ceremony
Maybe fifty
Mostly older people

The world forgetting

A THING OF BEAUTY

When the rapture comes, grab my foot
And we'll take a trip to Lilliput
Where we'll be big cuz the people are small
And God Himself is only two feet tall

When the rapture comes, grab my schnoz
And we'll take a trip to the land of Oz
Where the Wicked Witch is not very scary
And the Wizard himself is ordinary

When the rapture comes, grab my hand
And we'll take a trip to Wonderland
Where there's no stain on the White Rabbit's crotch
And time has stopped on the Mad Hatter's watch

When the rapture comes, grab my wrist
And we'll take a trip to the land of myths
Where Odysseus yearns for wife and home
And Penelope's yarn spins Homer's poem

When the rapture comes, grab my cock
And we'll take a trip to the land of schlock
Where once in a while by mostly luck
A thing of beauty can be snuck

BOOGER ON A ROCK

When the rapture comes, so will
The unexpected. For example:

I flick a booger on a rock
Just to watch it dry
But it grows wings and soars aloft
And right before my eyes
What I had thought a lump of snot
Becomes a boogerfly

AND DID THOSE FEET

When the rapture comes
Mississauga will disappear
As will Brampton
And any other burbs
Here on the cutting edge
Of Western civilisation where
Houses look the same
On streets that look the same

Here no dark satanic mills
Nor great godly feet

Here nothing happens except
The occasional suicide
Usually by a man who has
Killed his wife and kids
Or his neighbour's wife and kids
Because he wanted something
Different

THE SPARROW

When the rapture comes, the sparrow
Will not fall. In the meantime, in this mean
Relentless time, it is hit by a car
When it flies too low and only its mate
With frail, protective, outstretched wing
Stands watching over it in the road

PERFECT VISION

When the rapture comes, the world
Will be a better place: the earth will begin
Turning in the opposite direction, the new
Day will start in the evening and end
With a spectacular sunset in the East
The Gulf Stream will warm the beaches
Of Nova Scotia, there will be plenty of water
In California, things will taste like they
used to, itsy-bitsy spiders will stop climbing up
Water spouts, the moon will be closer and its
Smoother, glowing complexion will make
It look young for its age. I myself will look
Young for my age and stand six feet tall
With rippling muscles and a bigger penis
My shoulders will be broad again, my thighs thick
My vision perfect
Also my poems will have much, much
Deeper meaning and be loved by everyone
Forever and ever
Amen

JODI PARKER

When the rapture comes
Jodi Parker and I will sneak upstairs
To her parent's bedroom closet
Steal inside and close the door
Carefully
So as not to make a sound
And there, facing each other
On our knees amid the smell of shoes
And her mother's hanging dresses
The electric shock of her lips
Will once again course through me
And this time
Instead of opening the closet door
In our astonishment
As quickly as we could
I will hold her thickened shoulders
And stroke her long grey hair

DEJA VU

When the rapture comes, Jennifer
Is the girlfriend I want to see
The way she looked when
We were in our twenties
That time she walked towards me
With that swagger a beautiful woman
Has when she knows you're watching

High-breasted, long-limbed
Sunlight flashing off her teeth

My fear is, walking towards me
On some street in Seventh Heaven
She'll be the same age as me
Same gray hair, same wrinkled skin
Same look of disappointment
In her eyes

FOR THE FUTURE TO BEGIN

When the rapture comes
That Acadian teenage girl
Will be so disappointed

See how she walks across
Mabou beach here in Cape Breton

Ass undulating
Thigh muscles smooth and taut
Tummy flat with just a hint
In her lower abdomen
Of the womb she's carrying
And the two Fallopian tubes
Waiting on either side
With outstretched arms

For one of those boys running
Suddenly around like a bunch
Of French Revolutionaries
With their heads cut off

Waiting for the future to begin

ESPECIALLY AMBER

When the rapture comes
I want my cats

All of them

Especially Amber
Who is dying and who the vet
Will have to put down
First thing tomorrow morning

It is 2:00 A.M. and
I am sitting with her
She is lying on her side
On the bathroom floor

She is so thin I can feel
every bone beneath her skin

I have prepared a hole for her
In my backyard beside her mother

And her sister

I don't know what happened
To her brothers

Probably eaten by coyotes

Basil so toothless he could
Not have defended himself

Sam so weird he might have
Merely wandered off

A family of congenital loners
Ungrateful, demanding, indifferent

Like myself

All of us given to inexplicable
Moments of affection

Especially Amber
Who is purring now

The author reads "Especially Amber" (1:37)
www.tinyurl.com/RecitesAmber

FRIENDS

When the rapture comes
We're going to have a big BBQ
In my backyard
All my friends will be there

So many I will have trouble
Remembering their names

The sky blue
The grass green
The sun shining

Everyone swimming in the river

Playing badminton using the net
I strung across the lawn

Eating the hamburgers
I have spiced to perfection

Drinking my vintage plonk

And afterwards everyone will
Sit around telling stories no one
Has ever heard before

And everyone will say
Witty intelligent things
Especially me

THE WORST THING

When the rapture comes
The worst thing that can happen
Is you get left behind

Find yourself stumbling from
The bathroom back to bed
In the ill-lit room you live in
In the basement of the building
Where you work as a janitor
Wondering why your friends don't call

Find yourself talking to the roaches in the wall
Silverfish in the sink
Your tongue methodically fingering
A cavity in one of your teeth
The tip of it tippy-toeing around the edges
Then suddenly diving
Ecstatically
Into the abyss

ON THE SKYLINE TRAIL

When the rapture comes you discover
You've been on the Skyline Trail

Boring mostly
The path straight and narrow
Grey gravel
Wedged between hackmatacks
Broken occasionally
By a spectacular view

Or a sudden panic

The crack of a branch
In the underbrush
Could be a startled moose
About to charge
Or a pack of coyotes
About to attack
As happened to that girl
A few years back

The cautionary tales of those
Who have gone before

It is forbidden to step off the path

Nevertheless you turn to admire
A mushroom or a feathered fern

Or drink from a mountain brook

Or you take a chance and walk a ways
In what is obviously an animal's tracks

Mostly you just plod along

Wondering how long the path is
Before you reach the end
Where you've been promised a vision
So stunning
It will take your breath away

EXCLOSURE

When the rapture comes
The ranger angels will build
An exclosure fence
To keep the self-righteous out

Like that woman
When we were walking
The Skyline Trail in Cape Breton
With our dogs

Which a sign had told us not to do

We must have passed fifty people
Not one of whom said anything negative

Well, a couple joked about
The fine we could get

A few stopped to chat and pat

Ten Japanese posed with our dogs
For photographs

But that woman!

Said we weren't allowed to have dogs
On the Skyline Trail

Said they were strictly prohibited

Said too bad if we couldn't leave
The dogs in the car for three hours
On a hot summer day

Said so what if we'd driven
Two thousand miles

Said we should just turn around
And go home...

A fence made of whirling swords
The self-righteous outside looking in

One step too many
Get a little too pushy
And the exclosure cuts you to shreds

MR. LUCKY

When the rapture comes
Mr. Lucky will be re-membered

It was just before bed time
And Mr. Lucky, as he did every night
Was out walking his two dogs
The dogs were on leashes
Those thin, fifteen foot retractable leashes
Neither of which he could see
In the dark
His dogs, I mean, not the leashes
When he decided to take a leak

As he was standing there
His hand holding himself out
In the dark
Which he couldn't see
His hand, I mean, not the dark
The dogs smelled a rabbit
And took off after it
Looping their leashes
Around his penis
Which he couldn't see
In the dark

The rabbit, I mean, not the penis

PROMOTED TO GLORY

When the rapture comes, you who
So often predicted it
Will be the most surprised

All those years of shoulder shrugging
Of head-scratching, of cringing apology
Of impatient penitents
Banging on the door
Demanding their money back
The house
The car
The prosthetic limbs
You said they'd never need again

All those years of dodging, weaving, hiding
Changing your name
Only to pop up
In some God-forsaken place
With your hair akimbo
And your eyes aflame
Lightning forking from your tongue

So many times
Even you lost faith

And just when you thought you could retire
Maybe spend the "rest" of your days
Living in one of those swanky houses
You got your wrinkled fingers on

The trumpet sounds, the sky opens
And you find yourself promoted to glory
Angels patting you on the back, ushering
You into the vast, white-washed dormitory
Where they have prepared your eternal cot

The author reads "Promoted to Glory" (1:37)
www.tinyurl.com/RecitesPromoted

MRS. BIRCH

When the rapture comes, Mrs. Birch
Will be one of the many meek

My best friend's mother, I still
See her fifty-five years later
Through a child's wondering
Ignorant eyes
Scrubbing her hardwood floors

Pail of sudsy water by her side
Hair tied back in a scarf
Plastic coverings on the furniture

Always on her hands and knees
No matter how often I came to play

When the rapture comes, Mrs. Birch
Will look at the splintering walls
The crack opening in the ceiling and
Give a gap-toothed, thick-lipped grin

Then she will get up off her knees
Remove the plastic coverings
And sitting back
In her gold-embroidered chair
A pillow propped behind her head
Inherit the dusty, dirty earth

SPIRIT CATCHER

When
The rapture comes

A man
Sitting in the driver's seat of his SUV

Cobwebs
Stitching his left arm
To the steering wheel
His ear to the headrest
Behind him

Silver spirit-catcher threads
Between his forehead
And the rearview mirror

Eyes missing

Cartilage missing
Where the end of his nose should have been

Lips
Pulled back in a rictus

Teeth
In remarkably good condition considering
All the junk food he used to eat

MANKIND WILL MEND ITS EVIL WAYS

When the rapture comes at the end of days
Mankind will mend its evil ways
No more gin, no more dope
No more sin, no more pope
No more blues, no more sad
No more news, no more bad
No more sick, no more pill
No more trick, no more kill
No more greed, no more stress
No more bleed, no more mess
No more lies, no more tears
No more eyes, no more ears
No more breath, no more time
No more death, no more sublime

CATHARSIS

When the rapture comes
What we mostly want to see
Is poetic justice

Divine retribution

We crowd around the cliff-edge
Of Heaven, jostling, bumping wings
Wondering who today's evil one will be

Last week it was Hitler
Begging for mercy

They always beg for mercy

We all laughed because we knew
He was nowhere near being tossed in an oven
Six million times

The week before that
It was the bastard who put
A bullet up Garcia Lorca's ass

I myself pulled the trigger of the gun
That punished that son of a bitch

Cathartic, really
From the Greek to purge
Hence Purgatory

For God is love
And an eye for an eye means
Hell can not last forever

Not even for Osama bin Laden
Whose turn today
It turns out to be

We push him off the ledge
For the three thousandth time

It is a pleasure to see him fall
His legs kicking, arms flailing, his body
Growing smaller and smaller
Until he lands with a tiny splatter
On the sidewalk

Like a gentle drop of rain

VENGEANCE

When the rapture comes, there are
Some people I will need to get even with

That bitch who said my poems
Were self-contradictory

That other bitch who refused
To teach me the secret art
Of making love
Even though I practically dictated
The essays that got her through
First year university

That bastard who stole
My Martin guitar

That other bastard who pretended
To be my best friend while
Seducing my ex-wife

My ex-wife

The bus driver who deliberately
Let me out at the wrong stop
In the middle of nowhere
In the middle of the night
In the middle of January
In Montreal

The editor at a national newspaper
Who gave my idea for a column
To someone else

The record producer who told me
That audio tapes of famous actors
Reading best-selling novels was not
Commercially viable

The list of my enemies is
Very, very long

The nice thing about Heaven is
There's plenty of time

CHOOSE

When the rapture comes, seraphs
Will sing with dybbuks and demons
Everybuddy will call everybuddy bro
Arabs will stop being anti-Semitic
Chinese will stop multiplying faster
Than the beads of an abacus

When the rapture comes, Whites
Will get to choose whatever colour
They secretly wished they were

When the rapture comes, Jews
Will get to choose between
Amnesia on the one hand and
A machine gun in the other

PARADISE ON EARTH

When the rapture comes
Two kinds of ex-communists
Will resurrect

Both agreed that in a just society
There could be no parasites
No social classes
No hierarchies
No privileged elites
That everyone should be a worker
Sharing in the nation's wealth
According to his needs

The first kind contained men and women
Of immense ability and modest needs

The second kind were equally able
But their needs were insatiable

The first kind thought communism
Was the best way to achieve
Paradise on earth

The second kind thought communism
Was the best way to achieve
Power

The first kind died young
Shot or ice-picked in the head

The second kind
Died in their sleep

THE WAYS WE DIED

When the rapture comes
Naturally
Some of us sit around
Discussing the ways we died

A guy called Watkin
For instance
Bragged he'd kicked the bucket
Singing hymns to the greater glory of God
While being burned at the stake alive

Everyone agreed that must have been awful

Not to be outdone
Those who had been drawn and quartered
Described what it was like having your guts
Piled up in a stinking stew on your chest

Of course we all sympathized
But the general opinion was
You were probably already dead
By the time the quartering came around

There was a nasty squabble between
A Jew who'd been gassed at Auschwitz and
A German who'd been shot in the abdomen

Oodles of victims of 9/11, the Black Plague
The Titanic, assorted no-name drownings
People who'd died in an avalanche
People who'd been eaten by animals

Everyone agreed that too would be awful

People who'd been eaten by cannibals

This triggering a serious theological debate
Concerning whose body one's flesh belonged to

And then old Joe McKennedy stood up

He'd been captured by a warlord
In Afghanistan and tied to the tread of a tank
Which, very slowly, had inched forward
Crushing first his toes, then his feet
Then his ankles, his shins, etc., etc. ...

It was amazing to see how well
He'd been put back together again
Although, frankly, he always flew with a limp

ANSWERED

When the rapture comes, all your questions
Will be answered

Okay, not all your questions

Not silly ones like
How many angels can dance on the head of a pin

Or, if God knows everything, does He know
What it's like to be ignorant

Or, if Christ's blood did not contain God's DNA
Was He really human

But important questions like
Why did I marry my first wife

And where did I put my damned glasses

And would I have been happier if I'd
Never gone to college

ODE TO JOY

When the rapture comes everyone
Sings the same familiar song, becomes
A host of choiring angels
Standing row on row
Stretching to infinity
Our mouths opening and closing
In unison
Like a school of fish
Our eyes following
God's baton
As it dances to the tune
Of Beethoven's Ode To Joy

Everyone is singing
Except Beethoven

His eyes are filled with tears
He is hearing the symphony he composed
For the first time

And it is even more perfect
Than he had hoped

HALLELUJAH

When the rapture comes, everyone sings
Ode To Joy for ten thousand years
Then, just to change things up a bit
At God's command
The holy host of choiring angels
Switches to Hallelujah by Leonard Cohen

Everyone is singing, all of us
Standing in a row
Our mouths opening and closing
Like a flock of birds
On a wire

Everyone is singing
Except Leonard

His eyes are filled with tears
His song more perfect
When there was room for doubt

THUGZ MANSION

When the rapture comes, the one song
No one sings is Thugz Mansion

Except, of course, Tupac Shakur
Who somehow wangled a divine dispensation
To a heavenly crib of his own

You can see him if you sneak in
Kicking it with Dr. Dre, drinking peppermint
Schnapps with Jackie Wilson and Sam Cooke
His feet up on a sofa
Listening to Billie Holiday
Michael Jackson and Marvin Gaye
Louis Armstrong
Leadbelly
Ma Rainey
Sonny Terry and Brownie McGee
Ella Fitzgerald
Robert Johnson
Aretha Franklin
Lena Horne

The list goes on and on

All of them guests
In Thugz Mansion

All of them made
In God's spitting image

HOW TO SWALLOW A POET

When the rapture comes, you will finally be able
To swallow a poet

It is easier than you think
And probably more pleasurable

We begin of course with the head

A poet's head is much smaller than you'd expect
That impression of immense size
Is mostly because of the hair

That is why it is always advisable to shave the head

Also, this would be a good time to remove
Any unnecessary impediments
Things such as glasses, ear rings, nose rings, etc
As these may get caught in the larynx and/or
Cause indigestion

Then slacken your jaw and simply let it unhinge

With the poet lying on his back, pull him
Toward you across the table and place
The head in your mouth

Then press your tongue against your upper palate
And crush the skull

Fortunately, most poets are soft-headed
So the brains quickly run out

Take time to savour the juices

De gustibus non est disputandum
But I've always found the brains
Of the great 19th Century Romantics
A little too sweet

I prefer the best of the 20th Century poets

Perhaps the sight of millions of world war dead
Is what gives their brains that bitter edge

But on to the shoulders

You will notice that these are sloped
And generally undeveloped

After all, we are eating poets here
Not wrestlers

However, if the shoulders present a problem
Disjoint the arms and save them for later

Once you've swallowed the shoulders
The rest, as they say, is a piece of cake
The ribs form a most convenient bolus
The abdomen goes down like an oyster
The buttocks are always a nice chewy treat

It's the genitals which can be quite unpredictable
They can add a dash of seaweed flavouring
Especially if your poet was female and young

But if he or she was an older poet, my advice

Would be to spit that bit into your napkin

Which leaves the legs

I like to disjoint them at the hips
And eat them separately

Crossed thigh bones, by the way
Is the sign to your waiter
That your meal is finished

I personally avoid the feet

But I've seen plenty of people
Sucking on a poet's toes
Who say they are delicious

DIVINE IMPROVIDENCE

When the rapture comes, there will
Have to be a strict accounting
A great stock-taking of God's creation
All things bright and beautiful
Subject to cost-benefit analysis

Plants and insects, for instance
The needless multiplicity of their species
Despite mankind's best efforts
To eradicate them

Not to mention fish

And birds

And reptiles
Most of which taste like chicken

Or the hard-scrabble alphabet of mammals
From aardvark to zebra

Most of which mankind
Is more successfully eliminating

Or stars, so obviously
Inefficient as a source
Of night-time illumination

So many and yet so dim

Some so far away it takes
Millions of years for their
Light to reach us

A few moons in geosynchronous
Orbit would accomplish the same thing

Of course, the Creator creates
That's His nature
That's what He does
Even in His sleep

Still, suppose a trillion stars disappeared
Along with their planets
And indigenous life-forms

Would they be missed?
Would He?

CAPE BRETON SQUARE DANCE

When the rapture comes
All hell breaks loose
A finger scrapes a string

The fiddle makes a moaning sound
The signal to begin

Then the fiddler's feet
Beat out the beat
We swing our partners round

We allemande to left and right
Everyone stomps the ground

With a whoop we kick
Our heels so quick
You'd think we're in a fight

And though our flicking shoes need room
We hold our partners tight

The rhythm changes
It's faster now
And fits the Highland tune

The heat has risen in the hall
A lady starts to swoon

Her partner holds her
By the shoulder
He looks around appalled

He thought he'd find a waiting chair
But none sit by the walls

We're panting, sweating
We need a rest
Yet we circle round the square

The caller left us long ago
The fiddler's on a tear

GOD IS NOT

When the rapture comes
The first thing you
Notice is that God
Is not a secular humanist

COELACANTH

When the rapture comes, if it comes
Right now
This minute
Before I can finish this poem

If the ceiling opens
And God's blood-crudded fingernail
Flicks me against the wall
Or sets me dancing
On the head of a pin

Then Darwin was wrong
About everything

And angels laugh at the coelacanth
Which swam with clumsy, leg-like fins
For God-knows-how-many million years
Merely to show us His grin

NO ROOM AT THE INN

When the rapture comes, there will be no
Separation of church and state
No private room at the inn
For private thoughts and private feelings

No privates, period

No room here
For poets or loners or crazies
Or anyone who would just like
To curl up with a good book

Interesting how easily
Fascists and Communists
And religious fanatics of all kinds
Fit in

What a blessed relief it must be
To be unburdened of all freedom

And now, how so at home they seem
Twirling their halos round their fingers
Leaning on their floor-length wings

Still, there's a few of us weirdos left
Magi hiding in a manger
Whispering how right Nietzsche was
About most men being sheep
How very wrong
About Him being dead

ANGEL WITH A CIGARETTE

When the rapture comes you'd think
The purpose of life would finally
Be revealed

That the debate would end
Between those who say
Pursuit of happiness
And those who say

Trial by suffering
I asked an angel with a cigarette
Dangling from his lips
What he thought the purpose was

He shrugged and said God
Worked in mysterious ways

Said a lifetime without death
Was the real eye-opener

UNORIGINAL SIN

When the rapture comes
And no leaf fades
When the river stops
And no child wades
You stare at where
You wore a watch
—That wrist of timeless skin!
Wondering what broke the blade
Before you could dig it in

In this garden
Where angels wing
Where no rose blooms
And no thorns sting
The Tree of Life
Shades everything

PARADISIACS

When the rapture comes
What you can't believe
Is the number of angels
Wandering the streets
Their hair unkempt
Their wings unpreened
Their eyes glassy and indifferent

Angel junkies for whom
Paradise is not enough

Paradisiacs yearning for a fix

You see them everywhere
Pissing in alleys and doorways
Sleeping in cardboard boxes
Sprawled across heating vents
Blocking the sidewalk

Homeless, friendless, eternally dissatisfied
You can't help but feel sorry for them
As you step over their bodies
And hurry on to meet your maker

AVANT-GARDE

When the rapture comes apart
The avant-garde will be behind it

In the back streets of Heaven
Poets of such exquisite introspection
Their works are incomprehensible
Even to themselves

In the back streets of Heaven
A statue of the Virgin Mary
Daubed with angel excrement

A crucifix stuck upside-down
In a vase of angel piss

Buddhist temples burning, swastikas
Scrawled on synagogues, graffiti
On the glans of minarets

Anarchists breaking windows, breaking
Wind in the middle of a hymn

Artist-angels flying into towers, splattering
Their guts against the sides of tall buildings

God Himself joining in
Smashing everything

AT ONE WITH ATMAN

When the rapture comes
If you don't like your body
You can have it removed

Pure spirit of Zen no-mind
At one with the universe
We are neti, neti
Neither this, nor that

Both not and not not
We are complete

Perfect
Beyond wanting to be perfect

Beyond wanting
Beyond poetry
Beyond words
We have climbed Jacob's ladder
And pulled it in

IN THE BEGINNING

When the rapture comes, the flesh
Will be made word again
History re-spooling itself
Like a movie in reverse
Children on toboggans
Sliding slowly uphill
People walking backwards
Across thresholds
While doors close in front of them
Lines of whooping sword-armed men
Rushing away from each other
Chariots pulling horses out of battle
A stone axe
Flying out of a Neanderthal's skull
Women sucking babies feet first
From the blood between their thighs
Birds losing their feathers
And then their wings
Gigantic reptiles growing smaller
Walking fish-like, awkwardly, across beaches
Into the sea
The sea disappearing
The sun disappearing
The universe collapsing in a last flash of light
Into the black hole of God's ear

ETERNAL RECURRENCE

When the rapture comes
Everyone will see the light
At exactly the same time
In exactly the same way
Thus ushering in an age of
Universal brotherhood and peace
And just when everyone agrees
That something tremendously
Transcendental, transformative
And transfiguring has occurred
Just when everyone is drying out
Their new-hatched wings and
Congratulating each other on
Having at last overcome their
Mutual hatreds and political
Conflicts in an unprecedented
Harmony of thought and feeling
Some knucklehead like me
Writes a poem about how much
He misses the smell of asparagus
When he pees and the whole
Damned world starts over again

LOVE AMONG THE RUBBLE

When the rapture comes
We scamper across the rubble
Hide behind the smooth square rocks

And in our panic rush
Some cut their hands and feet on sharp
See-through shards sticking upwards
In the dust

The sky is strange
It is suddenly blue and there is
Something in the middle of it

It is so bright it hurts my eyes
When I look at it

I believe I have shit myself

At least the children have made it safely
Back to the ledges inside the cave

I hope they have run deep into one
Of the tunnels on either side

No one knows how far they go
The shaman says they never end

My legs are wet and trembling

I pick up a handful of gray-white dust
And scrape away the stink

I stand with my spear-thrower
Poised above my shoulder

Also, I have my great-great-grandfather's knife
The one with the magic blade no one
Remembers how to make

I am ready

DRONE ANGEL

When the rapture comes, our guns we seize
And all God's drones, like swarming bees
Come tumbling out from heaven's lair
To fix a world beyond repair

High-tech angels with laser stare
We come in for the kill on a wing and a prayer
Below us, bad guys run or freeze
We bomb and strafe, spray gas on the breeze

Though towns disappear with hair-trigger ease
Unfinished business is what a drone sees
Some hide in the desert, some hide in Time's Square
Some try to surrender, arms in the air

Befouling themselves in utter despair
They sing the Lord's praises, their innocence swear
Or, confessing sins and falling on knees
They show us their hearts and we aim to please

About the Author

Born in Montreal in 1946, Max Layton now lives in Cheltenham, Ontario. He is the singer-songwriter son of Irving Layton. Leaving home at the age of 16, he worked at jobs ranging from being a logger in BC to laying track in Saskatchewan to writing for a tabloid magazine in order to put himself through university. Later, he owned a bookstore, managed a subsidiary of McClelland & Stewart and was the vice president of a bank before becoming a high school English teacher. He is the author of a novel and a book of short stories. This is his first collection of poetry.

Acknowledgements

I want to thank friends and family for taking the time to make the many suggestions which have improved at least some of these poems from the wretched state they were previously in. My loving stepmother, Aviva, spent hours on the phone with me going over the manuscript and debating practically every line. I am deeply indebted to Robert Priest, not only for his editorial eye but also for the inspiration of his work and personal example.

The following poems have been previously published:

"To Sing Another Villanelle": The Toronto Quarterly

"On The Skyline Trail": Lion's Head Magazine

"For The Future To Begin": Lion's Head Magazine.